Windsurfing

Contents

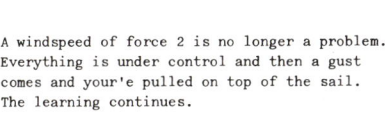

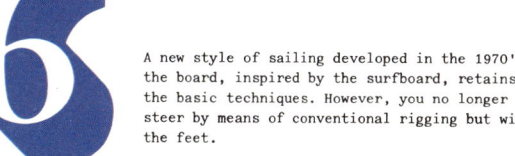
Text by Jean Luc Marty and Alexandre Bergevin / Artwork by René Deynis and Roland Garel / Scenario by Jeck

Also published by Corgi Books:
FOOTBALL
TENNIS
JUDO

WINDSURFING

A CORGI BOOK 0 552 542768

PRINTING HISTORY

First published in France by Chancerel Editions
Corgi edition published in Great Britain 1986

Copyright © in text and illustrations
Chancerel Editions 1984

Corgi Books are published by Transworld Publishers Ltd.,
61-63 Uxbridge Road, Ealing, London W5 5SA.

Printed in Italy by ROTOLITO LOMBARDA S.p.A., Milan, Italy

I

EQUIPMENT

THE WINDSURFER IS BASED ON A SIMPLE IDEA. IN HALF AN HOUR THE PRINCIPLES OF THE RIGGING CAN BE UNDERSTOOD. THEN, ALL THAT REMAINS IS TO LEARN TO SAIL THE BOARD.

WINDSURFING IS REPUTED TO HAVE BEEN INVENTED SOMETIME IN THE 1960s BY A CALIFORNIAN SURFER, HOYLE SCHWEITZER WHO MAY HAVE BORROWED THE IDEA FROM HIS COMPATRIOT, NEWMAN DERBY.

WINDSURFING IS A COMPROMISE BETWEEN SURFING AND SAILING, ITS DISTINGUISHING FEATURE BEING THE UNIVERSAL JOINT.

WITH THESE ARTICULATED COMPONENTS, ONE CAN CONTROL THE BOARD.

HERE, BY SIMPLE PRESSURE WITH THE FOOT, THE DAGGERBOARD PIVOTS ON ITS AXIS AND MAY BE PUT IN THREE POSITIONS.

HE RAISED HIS DAGGERBOARD.

YES, THAT'S A GOOD IDEA IN A STRONG WIND OTHERWISE THE BOARD SPINS OUT.

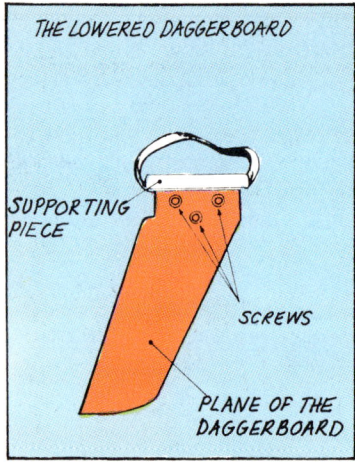

THE LOWERED DAGGERBOARD

SUPPORTING PIECE

SCREWS

PLANE OF THE DAGGERBOARD

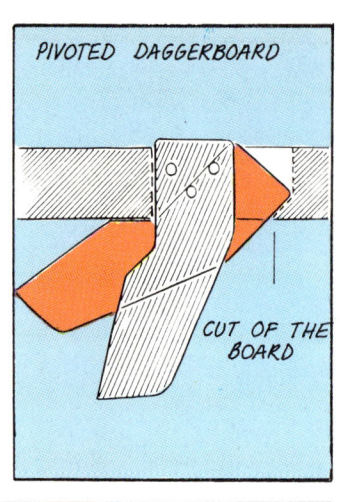

PIVOTED DAGGERBOARD

CUT OF THE BOARD

THANKS TO THE UNIVERSAL JOINT OF THE MAST FOOT THE SAIL MAY BE PUT IN ANY POSITION.

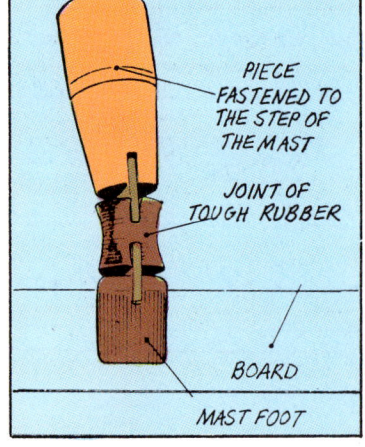

PIECE FASTENED TO THE STEP OF THE MAST

JOINT OF TOUGH RUBBER

BOARD

MAST FOOT

COMPLETE MAST FOOT WITH TRACK

WISHBONE

CLEATS - BINDING

MASTS ARE ALUMINIUM OR FIBREGLASS. THE WISHBONE IS A DOUBLE BOOM. THE INHAUL ATTACHES THE MAST TO THE FRONT OF THE WISHBONE AND AT THE OTHER END THE SAIL IS SECURED WITH THE OUTHAUL

THE UPHAUL

MY WISHBONE IS ALUMINIUM.

IT IS BEST CONTROLLED AT SHOULDER HEIGHT.

WHAT IS HIS SAIL MADE OF, ERIC?

POLYESTER. IT WEARS WELL SO LONG AS YOU ROLL IT, RINSE IT, AND DRY IT AFTER EACH USE.

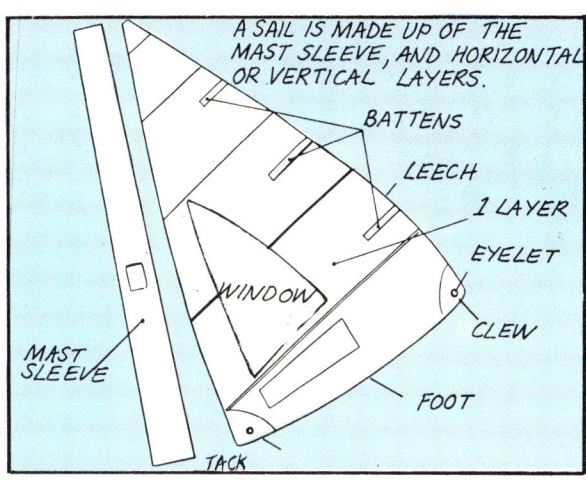

A SAIL IS MADE UP OF THE MAST SLEEVE, AND HORIZONTAL OR VERTICAL LAYERS.

BATTENS
LEECH
1 LAYER
EYELET
CLEW
FOOT
WINDOW
MAST SLEEVE
TACK

STORM SAILS WERE DEVISED TO PERMIT SAILING UP TO FORCE 7 OR MORE. ONE MAY ALSO USE THEM WHEN STARTING TO SAIL. THEY HAVE A SURFACE OF ABOUT ÷2m² TO 4·5m² AND ARE CUT DIFFERENTLY IN ORDER TO ALLOW THE WIND TO ESCAPE. THEY EITHER HAVE CONCAVE OR CONVEX LEECHES.

OTHERS HAVE A CONCAVE LEECH.

SOME HAVE CONVEX LEECHES.

IT REALLY IS FANTASTIC AT THIS SPEED!

FOR SAFETY, THE HARNESS (JACKET WORN AROUND THE CHEST) IS INDISPENSABLE WHEN THERE IS A LOT OF WIND.
ON LONG RIDES IT PLAYS THE ROLL OF A SUPPORTING TRAPEZE.

SHOULDER STRAP

SAFETY HOOK

TO TAKE OFF THE SAFETY HOOK, I MUST LOWER THE WISHBONE.

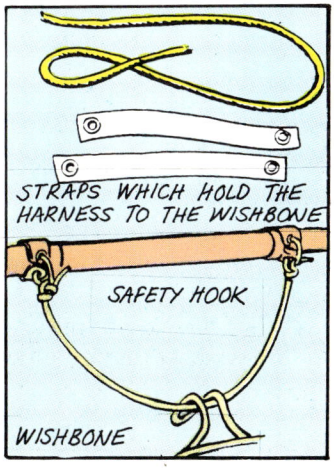

STRAPS WHICH HOLD THE HARNESS TO THE WISHBONE

SAFETY HOOK

WISHBONE

RIGGING HIS BOARD ONLY TAKES A FEW MINUTES

PUT THE END THROUGH THE EYELET OF THE SAIL AND INTO THE EYELET ON THE MAST FOOT.

THEN MAKE TWO HALF HITCHES

FINALLY, I PASS THE END AT THE EXTREMITY OF THE WISHBONE THROUGH THE EYELET OF THE SAIL.

TO ATTATCH THE WISHBONE TO THE MAST, YOU MUST PREPARE THE MAST. I'M DOING A ROLLING HITCH AROUND THE MAST AND A KNOT ON THE END TO SECURE IT.

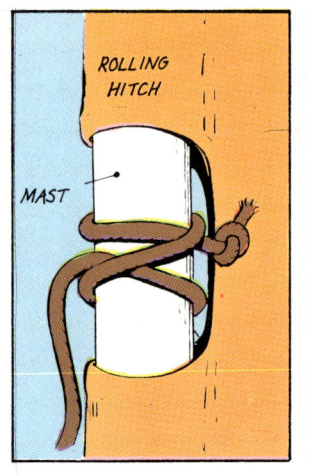

ROLLING HITCH

MAST

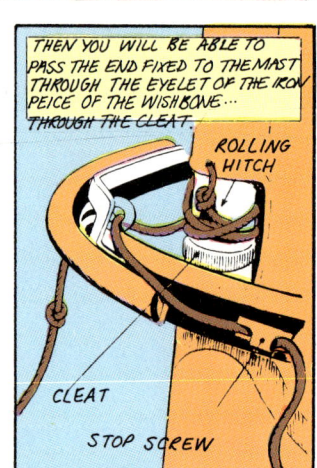

THEN YOU WILL BE ABLE TO PASS THE END FIXED TO THE MAST THROUGH THE EYELET OF THE IRON PEICE OF THE WISHBONE... THROUGH THE CLEAT.

ROLLING HITCH

CLEAT

STOP SCREW

AND YOU FINISH WITH TWO HALF HITCHES

SAFETY HOOK

SHOCK CORD

THIS IS WHAT ALLOWS YOU TO ATTATCH THE UPHAUL TO THE MAST FOOT.

UPHAUL

FINALLY, YOU MUST SLIP THE BATTENS INTO THEIR POCKETS AFTER HAVING CHECKED THEIR LENGTH.

2

THE FIRST TRY

FALLS ARE INEVITABLE ON THE FIRST TRY. THE ESSENTIAL THING IS THAT YOU UNDERSTAND THE BASICS. NEVER MIND THE FALLS: IT IS ALL PART OF LEARNING.

SO, THE MOST IMPORTANT THING IS TO BALANCE THE BOARD?

YES, YOU PLACE ONE HAND IN THE DAGGERBOARD SLOT AND THE OTHER ON THE EDGE OF THE BOARD.

NOW, I CARRY THE RIG TO THE WATER LIKE THIS... THE MAST CROSSWISE TO THE WIND.

CATHY, YOU MUST WASH THE MAST FOOT BY DIPPING IT INTO THE WATER

OH YES! TO PREVENT SAND FROM FALLING INTO THE MAST SOCKET.

NOW, LET'S PUT IN THE DAGGER-BOARD.

TO DO THIS YOU MUST BE FAR ENOUGH FROM SHORE OTHERWISE, GOING OUT YOU RISK BREAKING THE DAGGERBOARD

TO CATCH THE WIND YOU MUST BEAT. THAT IS TO SAY, NAVIGATE AT A 45° ANGLE TO THE WIND.

TO SAIL CLOSE TO THE WIND, YOU MUST KEEP THE SAIL AT THE LIMIT OF FLAPPING BY INCLINING THE MAST EITHER FORWARDS OR BACKWARDS, WHICH BEARS OFF OR LUFFS, ENABLING YOU TO BE AS NEAR THE WIND AS POSSIBLE.

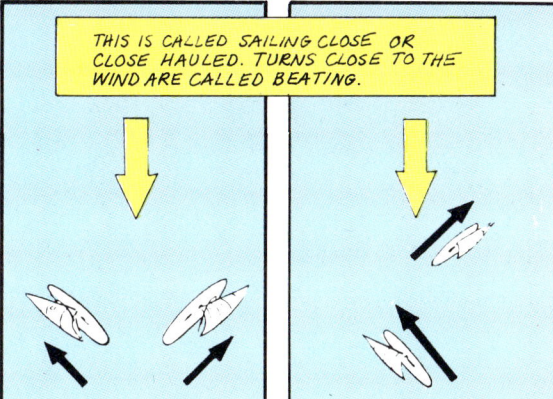

THIS IS CALLED SAILING CLOSE OR CLOSE HAULED. TURNS CLOSE TO THE WIND ARE CALLED BEATING.

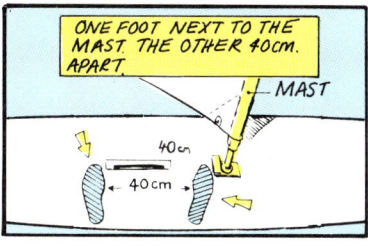

ONE FOOT NEXT TO THE MAST. THE OTHER 40cm. APART.

MAST

40cm
40cm

ONE HAND NEAR THE MAST, THE OTHER 40-43cm TOWARDS THE REAR OF THE WISHBONE.

WISHBONE

SAILING OFF THE WIND

BACK STRAIGHT, CATHY!

AND SHOULDERS LOW! I KNOW!

THIS SAILING TRIM IS USED IN A CROSSWIND AND IS BY FAR THE MOST FUN. THE FEET MUST BE PLANTED IN THE MIDDLE OF THE BOARD, THE LEGS APART FOR GOOD BALANCE.

IF THE WIND GROWS STRONGER, STRETCH OUT YOUR LEG IN FRONT AND SLIGHTLY BEND THE BACK LEG.

SAILING BEFORE THE WIND, YOU CAN'T COUNTERBALANCE THE PRESSURE OF THE WIND BY BRINGING IN THE SAIL; IT IS NECESSARY TO REPOSITION YOUR FEET TO MAINTAIN A VERTICAL POSITION TO THE SAIL. IF YOU MOVE THE LEG OPPOSITE THE WISHBONE SLIGHTLY FORWARDS OR BACKWARDS, YOU CAN KEEP YOUR BALANCE.

OH! OH! THE TRIM IS DIFFICULT TO CONTROL!

THE CENTRE OF MY SAIL MUST BE VERTICAL TO THE AXIS OF THE BOARD.

YOU SEE... EACH DIRECTION IN RELATION TO THE WIND CORRESPONDS TO A DIFFERENT SAIL SETTING.

HOW MANY TRIMS ARE THERE?

AM I ALWAYS AT THE LIMIT OF THE WIND?

IF I GO UP TO THE MAXIMUM AGAIN MY SAIL WILL START FLAPPING ALONG THE MAST.

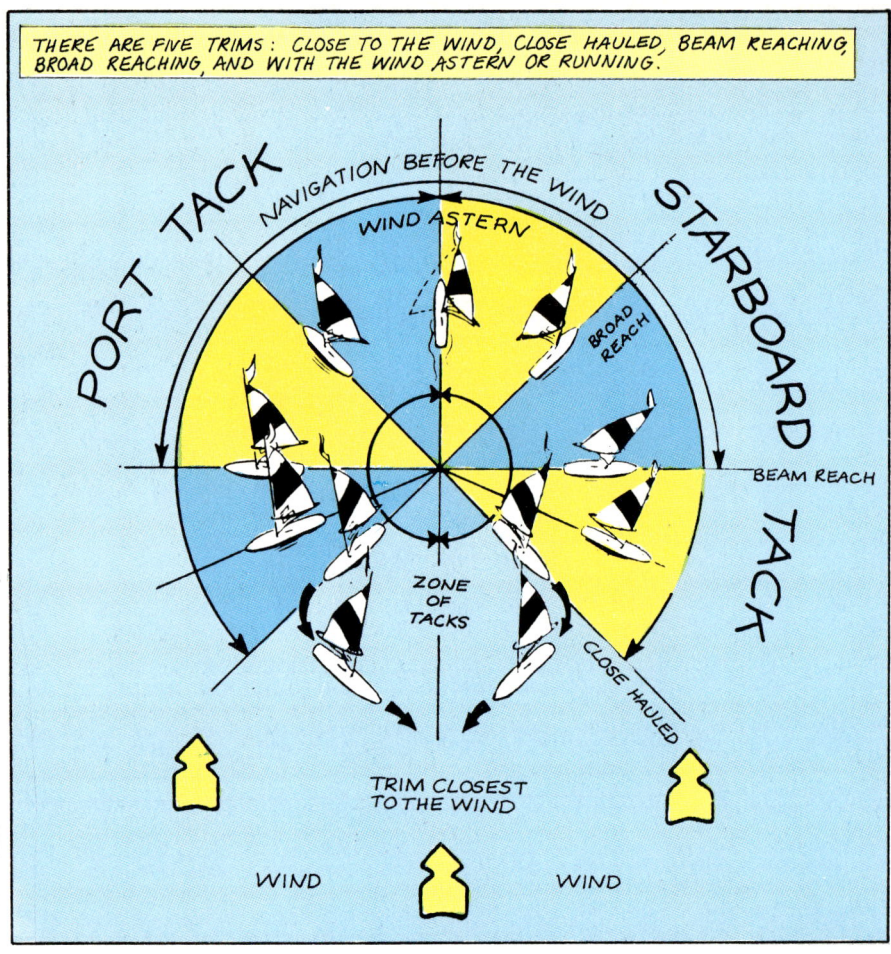

THERE ARE FIVE TRIMS : CLOSE TO THE WIND, CLOSE HAULED, BEAM REACHING, BROAD REACHING, AND WITH THE WIND ASTERN OR RUNNING.

PORT TACK

STARBOARD TACK

NAVIGATION BEFORE THE WIND

WIND ASTERN

BROAD REACH

BEAM REACH

ZONE OF TACKS

CLOSE HAULED

TRIM CLOSEST TO THE WIND

WIND   WIND

SAILING TO WINDWARD IS BEATING.

YOU PULL THE MAST THIS WAY TOWARDS THE REAR, AND YOU MOVE YOUR FEET AND THE WEIGHT OF YOUR BODY BACKWARDS. THESE MOVEMENTS MAKE THE BOARD LUFF. (THE BOARD FOLLOWS A CURVE INTO THE WIND). BUT BE CAREFUL! IT IS BEST TO KEEP YOUR FEET IN THE CENTRE OF THE BOARD.

LUFFING

I'M PULLING THE RIGGING TO THE FRONT.

CATHY IS GETTING READY TO BEAR AWAY. THAT IS, TO SAIL OFF THE WIND. SHE IS GOING TO INCLINE THE MAST TOWARDS THE FRONT OF THE BOARD. NOTICE THAT THE POSITION OF HER FEET, AT FIRST ENABLES THE WEIGHT OF HER BODY TO INFLUENCE THE FRONT.

MY BOARD BEARS AWAY WITHOUT ANY PROBLEMS.

TO START, YOU MUST ... KEEP THE MAST VERTICAL ... THEN CROSS YOUR HANDS. ONE HAND STAYS ON THE UPHAUL, THE OTHER IS CROSSED OVER AND POSITIONED AT THE FRONT OF THE WISHBONE. THE BODY WEIGHT MUST PROVIDE BALANCE TO COUNTERACT THE WIND IN THE SAILS.

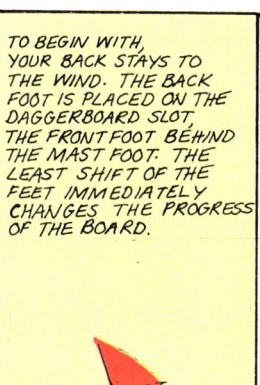

TO BEGIN WITH, YOUR BACK STAYS TO THE WIND. THE BACK FOOT IS PLACED ON THE DAGGERBOARD SLOT, THE FRONT FOOT BEHIND THE MAST FOOT. THE LEAST SHIFT OF THE FEET IMMEDIATELY CHANGES THE PROGRESS OF THE BOARD.

THE FRONT HAND HOLDS THE RIGGING, THE BACK HAND CONTROLS THE TENSION ON THE SAIL.

BACK STRAIGHT, BODY BRACED TO RESIST THE PULLING.

OH! THINGS ARE GOING BADLY!

LEANING FORWARD MEANS YOU'RE OFF BALANCE!

THERE ARE FOUR POSITIONS FOR VARYING THE GRIP ON THE WISHBONE AND FOR AVOIDING FATIGUE.

CLASSIC POSITION

OFTEN USED POSITION

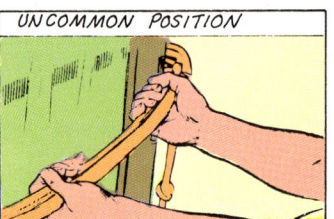

UNCOMMON POSITION

LEAST COMMON POSITION

TACKING ENABLES YOU TO SWING THE SIDES ONE WAY OR THE OTHER TO BEAT WINDWARD. CATHY HAS LEFT A CLOSE HAULED TRIM THEN LUFFED TO STEER TOWARDS THE WIND. THEN SHE BEGAN HER TACK BY HAULING THE SAIL TAUT. THE BOARD IS POINTING UPWIND. CATHY GOES AROUND THE MAST WHILE THE SAIL FLAPS AND THE BOARD CONTINUES TO TURN.

JIBING CONSISTS OF TURNING WITH THE WIND ASTERN WITHOUT PASSING IN FRONT OF THE MAST.

THE REAR HAND RELEASES THE WISHBONE, THE FRONT HAND CATCHES THE UPHAUL.

THE FORMER REAR HAND SEIZES THE OTHER SIDE OF THE WISHBONE.

NOW I'VE MADE THE SAIL TAUT... AND I AM ON THE RIGHT COURSE.

3

FURTHER PRACTICE

A WINDSPEED OF FORCE 2 IS NO LONGER A PROBLEM. EVERYTHING IS UNDER CONTROL AND THEN A GUST COMES AND YOUR'E PULLED ON TOP OF THE SAIL. THE LEARNING CONTINUES.

WHEN BROAD REACHING IN A STRONG WIND, IT IS NECESSARY TO RAISE THE DAGGERBOARD, THEN TO GUIDE THE BOARD WELL ACROSS THE WIND.

LIGHTLY SWING THE MAST FORWARD, YOUR FRONT FOOT PLACED JUST BEHIND THE MAST.

SWING YOUR BODY BACKWARDS, FLEXED, THE AIM IS TO RESET THE SAIL IN ONE MOTION.

SAILING OFF THE WIND IN A BREEZE...

MY FRONT LEG IS BRACED AND READY TO KEEP THE BOARD UNDER CONTROL.

IN A STRONG WIND THE PROBLEM IS AVOIDING TURNING IN TO THE WIND.

MY ARMS ARE STRETCHED AS FAR AS THEY WILL GO. I AM COUNTERBALANCING BALANCING WITH MY ENTIRE BODY.

LIKE THIS, YOUR BOARD IS CONTROLLED AND TRAVELS FAST.

THE DOWNHILL TENSION IS LOW AND SO CREASES APPEAR ALONG THE LENGTH OF THE MAST.

CREASES

CLEW

MANOEUVRING IN A LIGHT WIND.

WHEN THE SAIL IS WEAK THE SAIL MUST GIVE MAXIMUM POWER. SO, IT IS NECESSARY TO WORK THE FACE OF THE SAIL WITH APPROPRIATE MANŒUVRES. IN A LIGHT WIND YOU MUST TENSION THE SAIL LOOSELY IN ORDER TO GIVE MAXIMUM POWER.

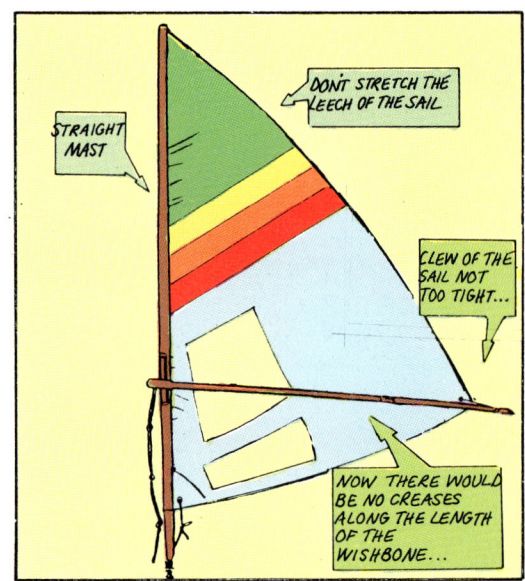

STRAIGHT MAST

DON'T STRETCH THE LEECH OF THE SAIL

CLEW OF THE SAIL NOT TOO TIGHT...

NOW THERE WOULD BE NO CREASES ALONG THE LENGTH OF THE WISHBONE...

THE WIND ESCAPES FROM THE LEECH.

THE MAST IS QUITE BENT.

THE HOLLOW ALONG THE MAST IS ABSORBED.

SECOND MANŒUVRE BELOW THE MAST.

MANŒUVRING IN A BREEZE.

ON THE OTHER HAND, IN A BREEZE, THE SAIL MUST BE FLAT TO ENABLE AIR CURRENTS TO FLOW THROUGH. YOU MUST HOIST THE SAIL TAUT ON THE MAST AND ON THE WISHBONE. THE BENDING OF THE MAST AUTOMATICALLY FLATTENS OUT THE SAIL.

END OF THE TACK

FLAT SAIL

SAILING CLOSE TO THE WIND WHEN IT IS STRONG, YOU MUST BRACE YOURSELF WITH YOUR ARMS AND RAISE THE DAGGERBOARD.

MAST LEANING INTO THE WIND...BODY HANGING OVER THE WATER... SKIMMING THE WAVES, THIS IS GREAT!...

THE WIND IS DYING DOWN... I'M GOING TO BEND MY KNEES AND LOWER MY CENTRE OF GRAVITY SO THAT I WILL NOT FALL IN.

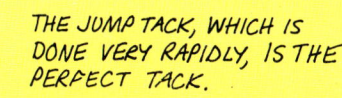

THE JUMP TACK, WHICH IS DONE VERY RAPIDLY, IS THE PERFECT TACK.

THEN YOU HAUL THE SAIL TAUT AND LUFF TO THE MAXIMUM. THE BOARD CHANGES DIRECTION. THE MAST IS SHARPLY PULLED BACKWARDS.

TO AVOID BEING SWEPT AWAY BY THE SAIL, I MUST VERY QUICKLY MOUNT THE LENGTH OF THE BOARD WHILE COMING ABOUT.

I AM QUICKLY SHIFTING MY WEIGHT TOWARDS THE BACK OF THE BOARD.

NOW, I AM UNDER THE NEW TACK.

THE SAIL REGAINS ITS SHAPE AND THE BOARD RESUMES ITS COURSE.

SAILING WITH THE WIND ASTERN, THE FEET MUST BE BEHIND THE DAGGERBOARD SLOT AND AS CLOSE TOGETHER AS FEASIBLE. BUT YOU MAY ALSO KNEEL.

I MUST BE CAREFUL ABOUT MY FEET!... THIS TRIM IS DIFFICULT.

I AM PULLING THE WISHBONE TOWARDS ME, BENDING THE MAST BACK. I HAVE RAISED THE DAGGERBOARD. MY BOARD MAINTAINS ITS COURSE.

TO JIBE IN A BREEZE YOU MUST HAVE THE WIND ASTERN UNTIL THE BOARD IS ABOUT TO HEEL OVER.

BE CAREFUL THE CHANGE WILL HAPPEN VERY QUICKLY.

AS SOON AS YOU RELEASE YOUR BACK HAND, THE MAST PIVOTS ON ITS AXIS.

WOW! THE SAIL JIBES ABRUPTLY BECAUSE OF THE WIND!

YOU MUST RECOVER THE SAIL VERY RAPIDLY BY INCLINING THE RIGGING BACKWARDS.

TO START FROM THE BEACH AND GO INTO THE WAVES, YOU MUST HOLD THE PIN UNDER THE LEFT ARM KEEPING YOUR RIGHT HAND ON THE MAST, GOING INTO THE WIND. FINALLY, THE FRONT HAND MUST BE READY TO OPERATE THE WISHBONE...

SLIDE THE FRONT OF THE BOARD INTO THE WAVES... CONTROL THE BOARD IN THE SWELL.

FROM THE TIME YOU GET INTO PROPER WAVES, YOU SHOULD PUSH THE REAR OF THE BOARD WITH A SNAP OF THE WRIST, LET THE BOARD SLIDE, GUIDED BY THE LEFT ARM THEN...

AND UP! I JUMPED ON THE BACK OF MY BOARD AFTER THE FIRST WAVE CREST PASSED.

19

4

REGATTAS

RACING IS A SPORT WITH ITS OWN RULES: ONE DOES NOT START HAPHAZARDLY. FOR EXAMPLE, TO WHICH SIDE OF THE BEAT DOES THE LEADING GROUP GO TO REACH THE WINDWARD MARK? WHAT TACK DO YOU HAVE TO CHOOSE TO LEAD THE GROUP AND TO BE FIRST AROUND THE WINDWARD BUOY?

THE RACE COMMITTEE RAISES THE YELLOW FLAG OF THE SERIES TEN MINUTES BEFORE THE START OF THE RACE.

THE OLYMPIC COURSE IS MADE UP OF TWO PARTS. THE FIRST PART IS REPRESENTED WITH A TRIANGLE REQUIRING A BEAT FOLLOWED BY TWO REACHES. THE SECOND ALSO INCLUDES A BEAT BUT TO IT IS ADDED A RUN. THEN A SECTION CLOSE TO THE WIND. THUS THE COURSE REQUIRES THE COMPETITORS TO GIVE THE MAXIMUM EFFORT TO ALL POINTS OF SAILING.

FLAG P.

FIVE MINUTES LATER THE COMMITTEE BOAT GIVES THE SIGNAL ANNOUNCING FIVE MINUTES UNTIL THE START.

THE FIVE MINUTE RULE (OR ONE MINUTE) IS SPECIFIED IN THE RACING RULE BOOK. IT INDICATES THAT YOU MUST BEGIN TO COMPETE FOR STARTING POSITION IN FIVE MINUTES OR IN THE ONE MINUTE BEFORE THE LAST CANNON SHOT.

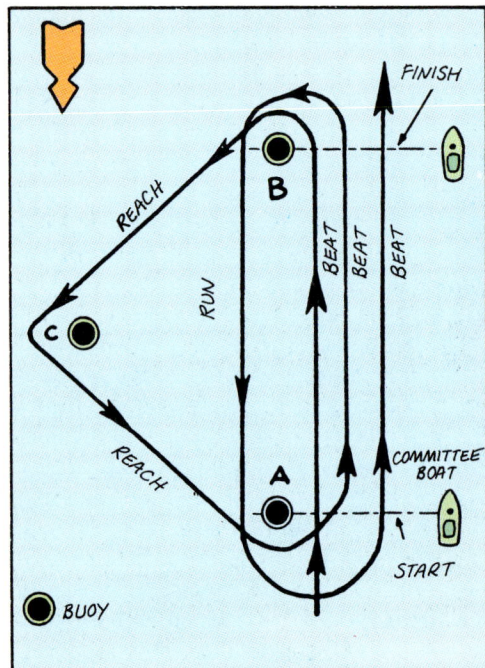

FINISH

REACH

B

BEAT BEAT BEAT

RUN

C

REACH

A

COMMITTEE BOAT

START

BUOY

BOUM!

THE STARTING LINE IS NOT
SET UP PERFECTLY
PERPENDICULAR TO THE
DIRECTION OF THE WIND,
IN ORDER TO GIVE EACH
BOARD AN EQUAL CHANCE
AT THE MOMENT
OF CROSSING THE LINE.

DOWN-
WIND

UP-
WIND

BEFORE THE START, THE
BUOYS ARE NOT
CONSIDERED THE MARKS
FOR THE COURSE.

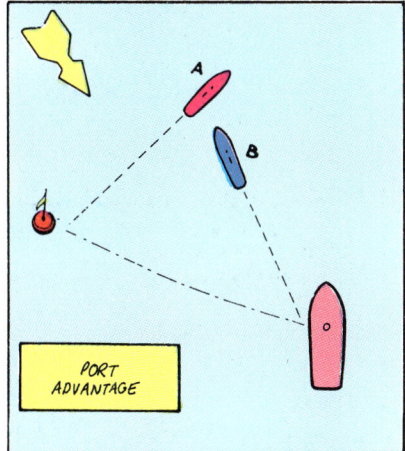

PORT
ADVANTAGE

PERPENDICULAR LINE TO WIND DIRECTION

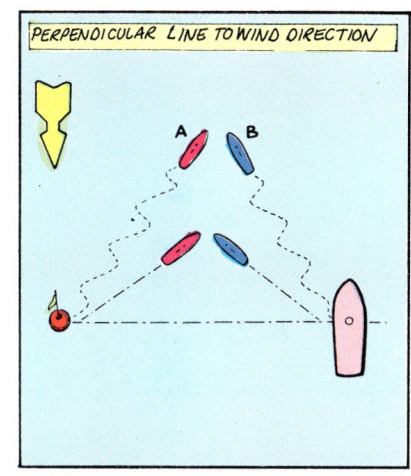

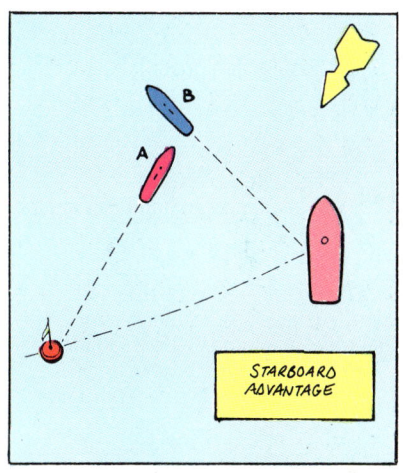

STARBOARD
ADVANTAGE

THE BEST WAY TO CHOSE THE
STARTING PLACE IS TO COMPETE
WITH ONE OTHER SAILOR.
HERE **A** AND **B** ARE TIED
BUT **B** HAS THE RIGHT OF WAY
OVER **A**. THUS HE HAS THE
BEST START. THE IMPORTANT
THING IS TO DISENGAGE
ONESELF FROM THE OTHER
COMPETITORS.

60236
STARTED TOO SOON!
I AM RAISING AN
ANSWERING PENNANT.
WE MUST HAVE A
NEW START!...
FIRE THE CANNON
AGAIN.

IRYU International Yacht Racing Union.

THE CONCEALED BOARD SAILS ON THE STARBOARD TACK AND THUS HAS THE PRIORITY OVER 60236

I MUST MOVE OUT OF THE WAY.

A BASIC RULE: A YACHT ON A PORT TACK MUST MOVE OUT OF THE WAY OF A YACHT ON A STARBOARD TACK, WHATEVER THE TRIM MAY BE. (Article 36 of the IYRU)

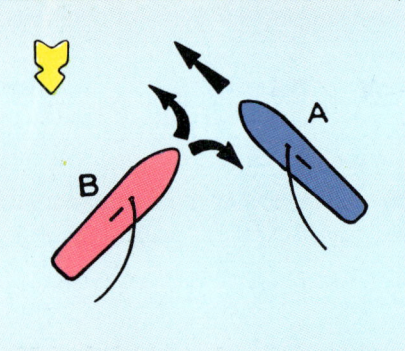

A NAVIGATES ON A PORT TACK AND MUST YIELD TO **B**, WHO NAVIGATES ON A STARBOARD TACK. (ALTHOUGH **B** HAS THE WIND ASTERN)

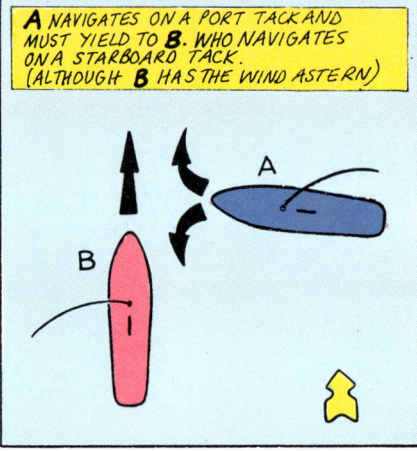

A YACHT WHICH ESTABLISHES AN OVERLAP TO LEEWARD FROM CLEAR ASTERN SHALL ALLOW THE WINDWARD YACHT AMPLE ROOM AND OPPORTUNITY TO KEEP CLEAR.

(Rule 37.3 of the IRYU)

A WINDWARD YACHT SHALL KEEP CLEAR OF A LEEWARD YACHT.

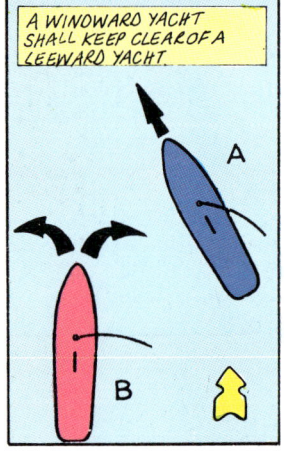

A YACHT CLEAR ASTERN SHALL KEEP CLEAR OF A YACHT AHEAD.

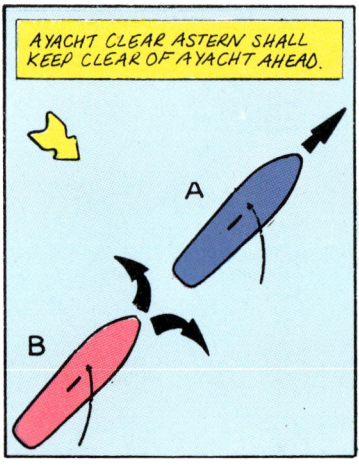

B IS ATTEMPTING TO OVERTAKE TO LEEWARD OF **A**. HE IS FORBIDDEN TO LUFF. (HE MUST FOLLOW HIS NORMAL ROUTE).

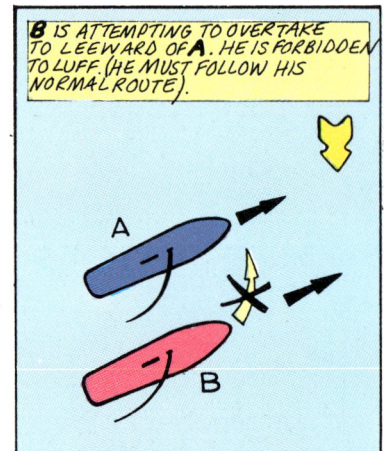

AN OUTSIDE YACHT SHALL GIVE EACH INSIDE OVERLAPPING YACHT ROOM TO ROUND OR PASS A MARK OR OBSTRUCTION.

B MUST LEAVE SUFFICIENT ROOM FOR **A** TO TACK.

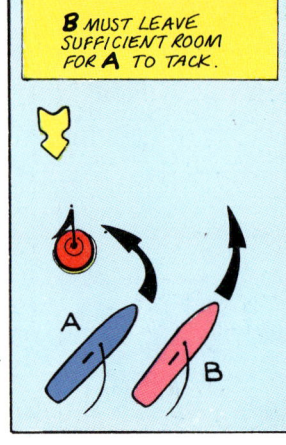

A HAS THE PRIORITY BECAUSE OF HIS STARBOARD TACK. (see Article 36).

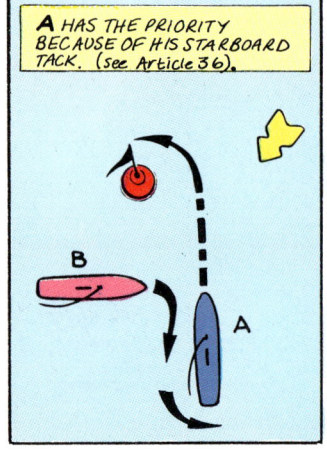

YACHT **A** IS ENTITLED TO ROOM AT THE MARK PROVIDED HE ESTABLISHES AN INSIDE OVERLAP WHEN YACHT **B** IS TWO BOAT LENGTHS FROM THE MARK.

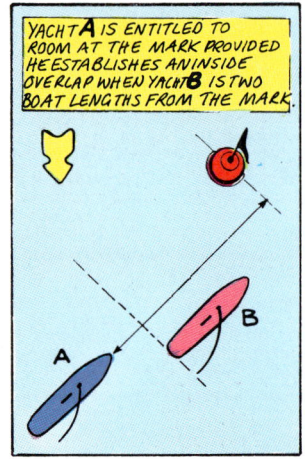

NOW IT IS IMPORTANT TO BREAK WELL AWAY FROM THE OTHERS!... AND NOT TO HAVE ANYONE TACKING YOUR WIND SO YOU CAN PASS WITHOUT OBSTRUCTION!

A: I AM BEING BLOCKED FROM THE WIND.

B: I MUST BREAK AWAY. I PREFER TO BEAR OFF RATHER THAN TO TACK BECAUSE C WOULD HAVE THE PRIORITY OVER ME WHICH WOULD FORCE ME TO PASS BEHIND HIM.

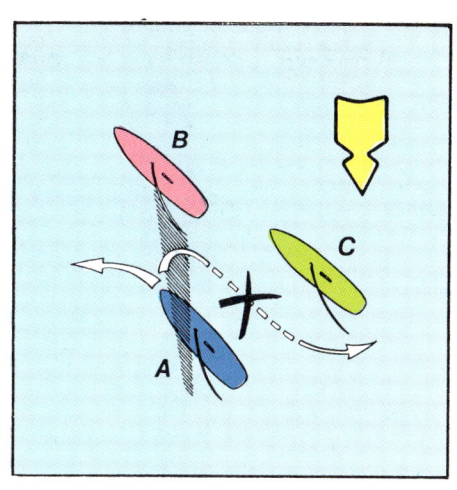

A: I AM BEING BLOCKED FROM THE WIND BY B. I MUST BREAK AWAY. I PREFER TO TACK BECAUSE NO ONE IS HINDERING ME.

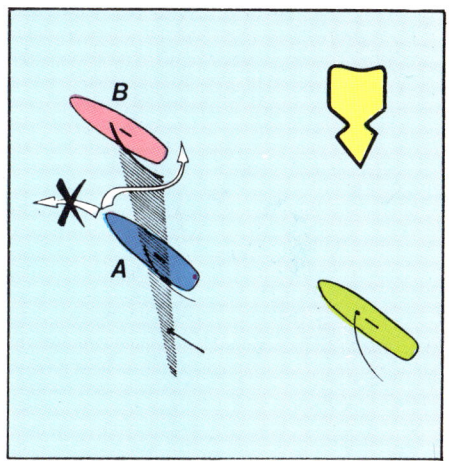

WHEN APPROACHING A BUOY TO LEEWARD (AND IF YOU ARE BEING CHALLENGED) YOU MUST ASK THE OTHER RACERS FOR WATER AND THEY ARE OBLIGATED TO GIVE YOU WATER TO TACK.

THIS MANŒUVRE CAN WIN YOU PLACES.

IT IS BEST TO HEAVE TO IN ORDER TO BE ON THE SAME TACK.

WHAT IS MOST COMMON IN A REGATTA ON THE REACHES, IS TO DEVELOP AN ATTACK TO WINDWARD. B LUFFS TO AVOID BEING OVERTAKEN TO WINDWARD. IT IS A LUFFING MATCH.

A IS ON THE PORT SIDE. HE MUST GIVE WAY TO B AND ALTER HIS COURSE.

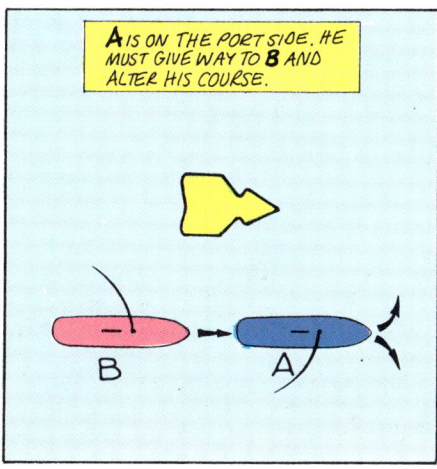

A AND B ARE ON THE SAME TACK. B MUST MOVE OUT OF A'S WAY. BECAUSE B IS TO WINDWARD.

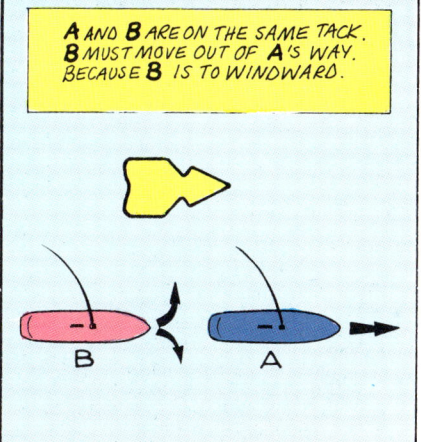

RELAY RACES ARE ALWAYS SPECTACULAR AND ENTERTAINING. THEY REQUIRE AT LEAST TWO BUOYS TO LEEWARD AND ONE CLOSE TO THE WIND. EACH TEAM IS MADE UP OF TWO SAILORS WHO TAKE TURNS RACING THE BOARD.

THEY START FROM THE BEACH, THE RIGGING SET UP. THE COMPETITOR WHO STAYS BEHIND HELPS HIS TEAMMATE START.

START

PASSAGE

BULLETIN BOARD.

AFTER HAVING FINISHED THE FIRST LAP, THE TEAMMATE WHO SAILED RUNS UP THE BEACH TOWARDS THE ENTRANCE OF THE PASSAGE.

NOW I AM GOING TO RETURN MY BLUE CHIP, TAKE ANOTHER COLOUR AND PASS IT TO MY TEAMMATE.

YOUR TURN! GO!

THE RACE ENDS WHEN THE FIRST RACER ARRIVES AT THE BEACH, OR THE NUMBER OF LAPS SCHEDULED HAVE BEEN COMPLETED. EACH MUST END THE LAP WHICH HE STARTED.

THIS IS AN ALTERNATIVE FORM OF RACE. THERE ARE FOUR MARKERS ON THE COURSE.

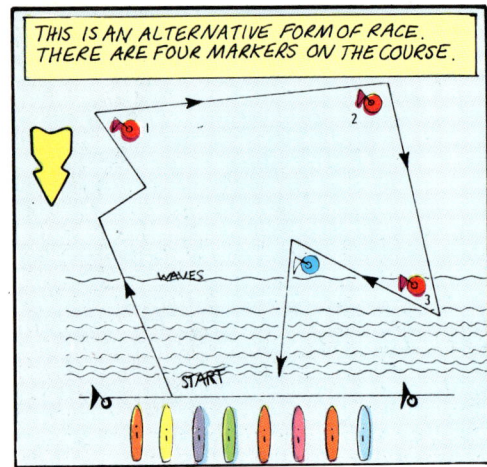

WAVES

START

ONE BEAT IS IN THE SURF. FROM THE START YOU HEAD FOR THE BUOY TO WINDWARD THEN YOU TACK ON TO A CLOSE REACH TO GO TO BUOY NO.2.

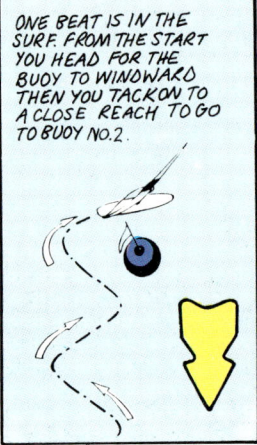

... BEAR AWAY ON TO A BROAD REACH AND HEAD FOR BUOY NO.3.

5

FREE STYLE

THIS IS THE MOST AESTHETIC FORM OF WINDSURFING A COMBINATION OF RHYTHMIC MOVEMENTS, FREE STYLE EPITOMISES THE TECHNICAL AND ARTISTIC POSSIBILITIES OF THE SPORT.

TO SUCEED IN A JUMP TACK: BOARD FLAT... BRUSH THE SURFACE OF THE WATER WITH THE WISHBONE...

GET READY! IT WILL SOON BE TIME TO LEAP WITH BOTH FEET!

OH!

THE TACK IS FINISHED! I MUST CORRECT THE POSITION OF MY LEGS... MY RIGHT FOOT SHOULD BE PLACED...

...BEHIND THE MAST AND THE LEFT ONE SLIGHTLY TOWARDS THE REAR.

TO EXECUTE THE HEAD-DIP, LOWER THE TORSO, BENDING IT BACKWARDS...

AND TO PLUNGE THE HEAD INTO THE WATER!

ON THE RAILRIDE YOU MUST START OFF THE WIND AND BEAR OFF SLIGHTLY.

THE LEFT FOOT PERCHES ON THE BOARD. NOTICE THE POSITION OF THE RIGHT FOOT WHICH WILL HELP RAISE THE BOARD.

I MUST NOT RISE AGAIN ESPECIALLY AGAINST THE WIND!

ON THE RAILRIDE, THE BOARD HAS A TENDENCY TO LUFF... I MUST RAISE MY CENTRE OF GRAVITY

WATCH OUT! LUFF! THIS IS BECOMING DELICATE!

OPEN THE SAIL TO BEAR OFF A LITTLE.

ERIC MOUNTS THE RAIL OF THE DAGGERBOARD. THE BOARD IS WELL OFF THE WIND...

THUMBS OVER THE WISHBONE.

I OPEN THE SAIL AND AT THE SAME TIME I PUT BOTH FEET ON THE DAGGERBOARD.

TO BEGIN A BACK TO SAIL, YOU MUST KEEP THE SAME TACK.

YOUR FRONT LEG IS SHIFTED TOWARDS THE FRONT BESIDE THE MAST FOOT.

LOOK AT THE ARRANGEMENT OF ERIC'S FEET AND THE MOVEMENT OF HIS ARM.

THE RIGHT HAND ON THE MAST IS TO LUFF OR BEAROFF AT WILL... THE LEFT HAND CONTROLS THE SAIL.

THE START IS SIMILAR TO A BACK TO SAIL BUT THE FEET ARE SHIFTED TOWARDS THE FRONT.

THE HAND ON THE CLEW BECOMES THE MAST HAND AND THE MAST HAND BECOMES THE CLEW HAND UNDER THE WIND.

WHEN YOU PIVOT TO PUT YOUR CHEST AGAINST THE SAIL, THE FRONT FOOT BECOMES THE BACK FOOT.

FOR THE PIROUETTE I MUST TURN MYSELF AROUND AND THEN GRASP THE WISHBONE IN A NORMAL POSITION...

OK! I HAVE RECOVERED THE WISHBONE IN A NORMAL POSITION.

ERIC TURNS AROUND: THE HAND WHICH WAS ON THE MAST CONTROLS THE WISHBONE AS LONG AS POSSIBLE.

FOR THE SWALLOW YOU MUST TAKE CARE THAT THE BOARD IS PERPENDICULAR TO THE SAIL.

BE CAREFUL AT THE START AGAINST THE WIND!

IT IS BEST TO AVOID DOING THIS IN A SQUALL OR WHEN THE WIND IS BLOCKED BY ANOTHER SAILOR.

I MUST AVOID PUSHING THE MAST TO ONE SIDE; OTHERWISE I MAY FALL!

MY BODY AND THE SAIL REMIND ME OF A SWALLOW'S WINGS! THEY FORM AN ATTRACTIVE SHAPE.

THIS POSITION IN THE WISHBONE IS SIMPLE BUT SPECTACULAR.

THE TOP OF MY TORSO COUNTERBALANCES AND ALLOWS ME TO TACK OR NOT...

IF THERE IS A LOT OF WIND, IT IS ENOUGH TO FLEX THE LEGS...

I AM LEANING AGAINST THE WISHBONE WITH ALL OF MY WEIGHT.

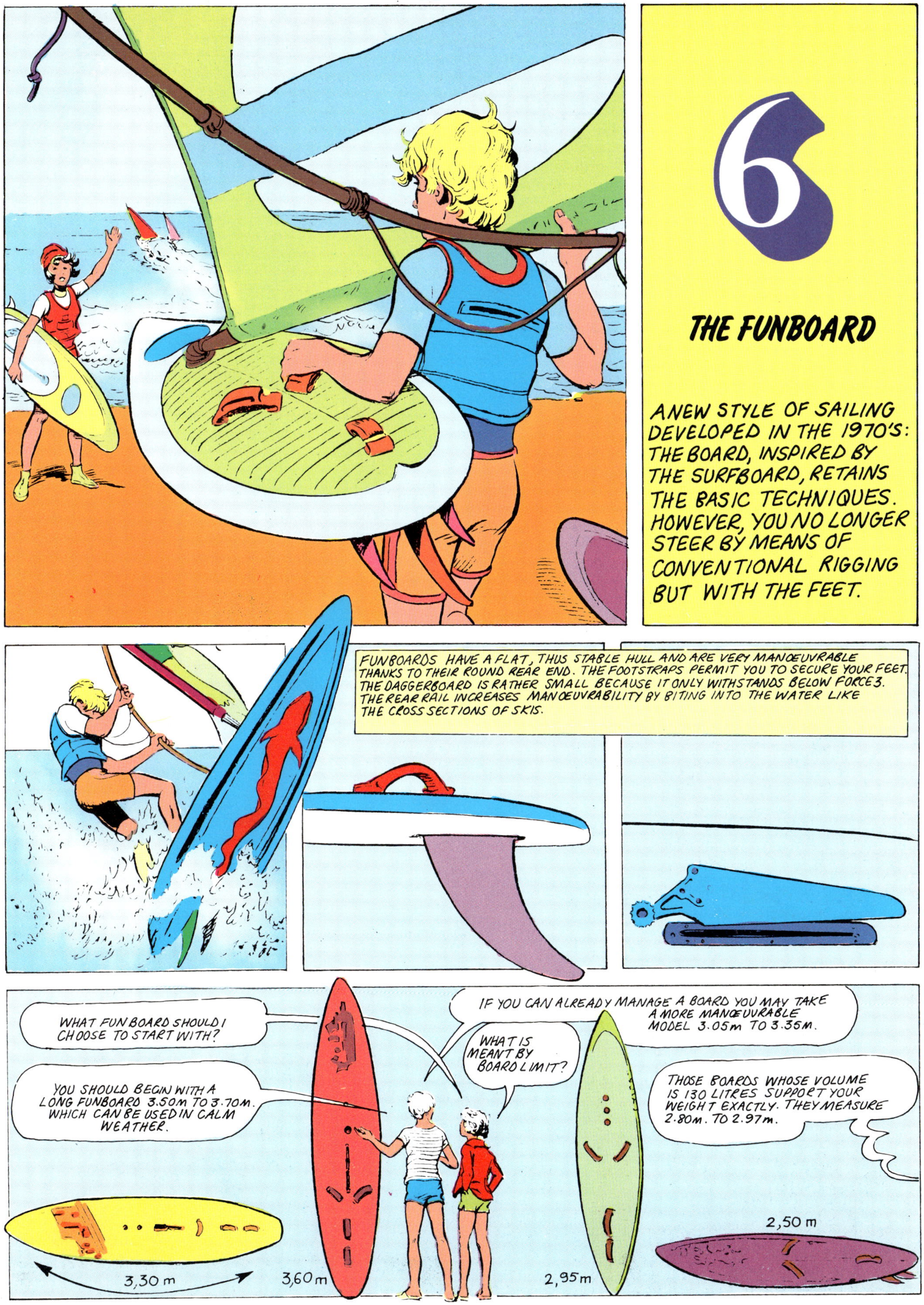

THE FUNBOARD

A NEW STYLE OF SAILING DEVELOPED IN THE 1970'S: THE BOARD, INSPIRED BY THE SURFBOARD, RETAINS THE BASIC TECHNIQUES. HOWEVER, YOU NO LONGER STEER BY MEANS OF CONVENTIONAL RIGGING BUT WITH THE FEET.

FUNBOARDS HAVE A FLAT, THUS STABLE HULL AND ARE VERY MANOEUVRABLE THANKS TO THEIR ROUND REAR END. THE FOOTSTRAPS PERMIT YOU TO SECURE YOUR FEET. THE DAGGERBOARD IS RATHER SMALL BECAUSE IT ONLY WITHSTANDS BELOW FORCE 3. THE REAR RAIL INCREASES MANOEUVRABILITY BY BITING INTO THE WATER LIKE THE CROSS SECTIONS OF SKIS.

WHAT FUNBOARD SHOULD I CHOOSE TO START WITH?

YOU SHOULD BEGIN WITH A LONG FUNBOARD 3.50m TO 3.70m. WHICH CAN BE USED IN CALM WEATHER.

WHAT IS MEANT BY BOARD LIMIT?

IF YOU CAN ALREADY MANAGE A BOARD YOU MAY TAKE A MORE MANOEUVRABLE MODEL 3.05m TO 3.35m.

THOSE BOARDS WHOSE VOLUME IS 130 LITRES SUPPORT YOUR WEIGHT EXACTLY. THEY MEASURE 2.80m. TO 2.97m.

3,30 m

3,60 m

2,95 m

2,50 m

THESE SAILS ARE VERY STREAMLINED

YES, THEY OFFER GREAT MANOEUVRABILITY.

THE NARROW FOOT OF THE SAIL PERMITS THE USE OF A SHORT WISHBONE WHICH WILL NOT HIT THE WATER DURING MANOEUVRES.

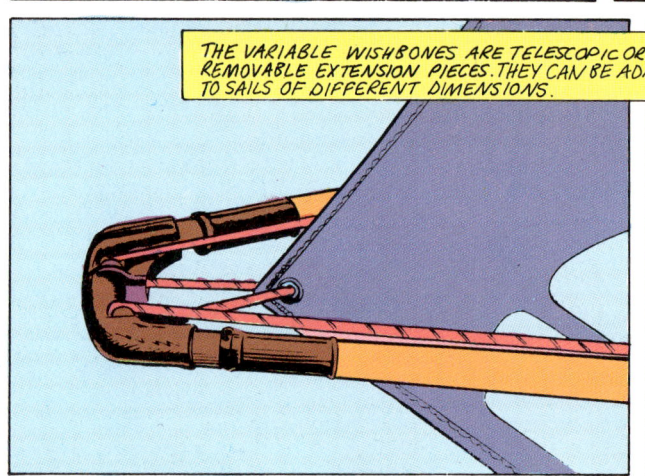

THE VARIABLE WISHBONES ARE TELESCOPIC OR HAVE REMOVABLE EXTENSION PIECES. THEY CAN BE ADAPTED TO SAILS OF DIFFERENT DIMENSIONS.

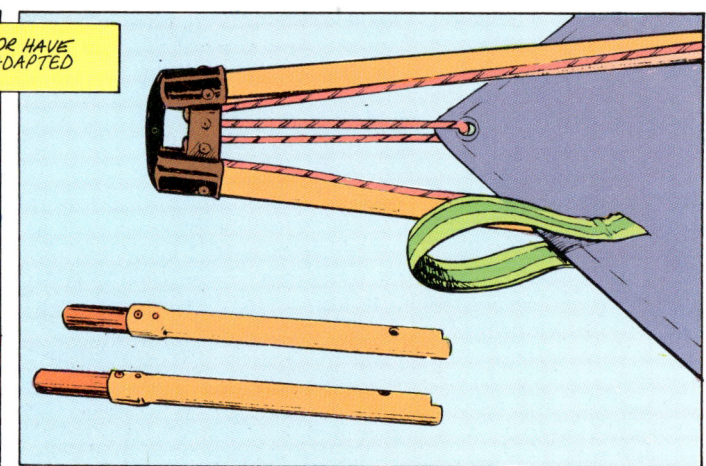

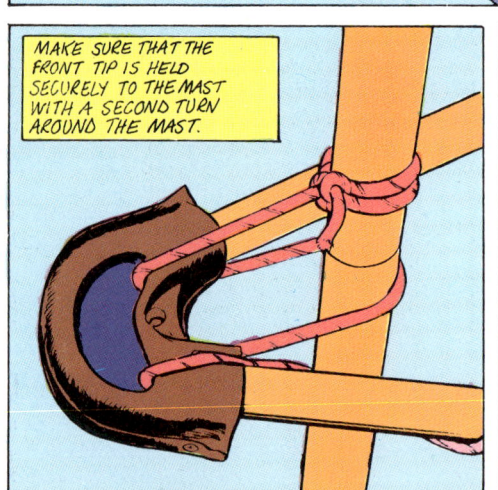

MAKE SURE THAT THE FRONT TIP IS HELD SECURELY TO THE MAST WITH A SECOND TURN AROUND THE MAST.

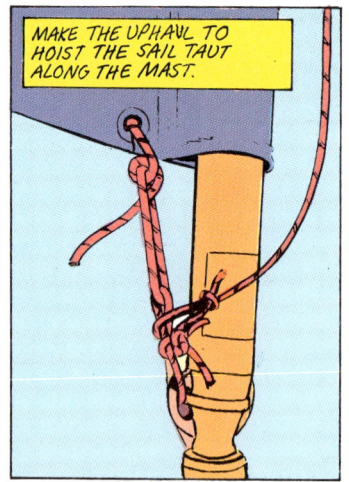

MAKE THE UPHAUL TO HOIST THE SAIL TAUT ALONG THE MAST.

YOU MUST PULL THE CLEW VERY TIGHTLY IN ORDER TO MAKE THE FOLDS DISAPPEAR. A FLATTENED SAIL IS EASIER TO HOLD IN A BREEZE.

THE TRACK PERMITS YOU TO CONTROL THE POSITION OF THE MAST FOOT.

THE MAST FOOT IS ADJUSTABLE WITH THE HAND.

THE MAST FOOT TRACK IS ADJUSTABLE WITH THE FOOT.

A FUNBOARD WITHOUT A DAGGERBOARD RISES CLOSE TO THE WIND WHEN YOU LEAN ON ITS REAR RAIL AGAINST THE WIND.

A LIGHT COUNTERLIST HOLDS THE DIRECTION AGAINST THE DRIFT.

YOU MUST WATCH YOUR SPEED WELL WHILE SEARCHING FOR A CLOSE-HAULED TACK.

IT IS LIKE SURFING, THE FEET DO EVERYTHING.

ON A FUNBOARD IN OVER FORCE 3 THE LATERAL SUPPORTS FOR THE FEET CAUSE IMMEDIATE RESPONSES (THE OPPOSITE OF THOSE OF A CLASSIC BOARD) THE LIST REQUIRES YOU TO BEAR OFF, THE COUNTER-LIST TO LUFF.

WHEN THE WIND BLOWS FROM THE SEA, YOU CAN SURF THE ROLLING WAVES TO LAND ON THE BEACH. BIGGER WAVES ENABLE YOU TO CARRY OUT SURFING MANOEUVRES.

YOU PULL ON THE FOOTSTRAPS TO LUFF.

OR LEAN ON YOUR TOES TO BEAR OFF.

A WAVE FORMS FROM BEHIND. YOU MUST WATCH IT.

THE WAVE ARRIVES. PUT YOURSELF PERPENDICULAR TO IT TO START THE SURF.

THE BOARD ACCELERATES. MOVE YOUR WEIGHT BACKWARDS TO AVOID WIPING OUT, FLEXING YOUR ARMS AND KNEES TO ABSORB THE SHOCK.

HOW CAN YOU MAKE A HALF TURN SO QUICKLY, ERIC?

BY EXECUTING A JIBE, CATHY.

AS SOON AS THE WIND IS ASTERN YOU MUST RECENTRE YOUR BODY WEIGHT, AND FLEX YOUR KNEES TO RETAIN YOUR BALANCE WHILE OPENING THE SAIL.

AT FULL SPEED BEGIN A FREE FALL LEEWARD WITH A STRONG GRIP ON THE CROSS SECTION.

MOVE THE FRONT FOOT AGAINST THE BACK FOOT, THEN PUT THE BACK FOOT IN FRONT AND LET GO OF THE...

WISHBONE WITH THE FRONT HAND AND GRAB THE MAST WITH IT.

TAKE THE WISHBONE WITH THE OTHER HAND. THEN SET OFF AGAIN.

FOR THE DUCK JIBE YOU BEAR OFF AS IT BEGINS TO JIBE, BUT WHEN THE WIND IS ASTERN, YOU TACK THE SAIL ON ITS AXIS.

YOU BEND BACKWARDS TO PASS UNDER THE SAIL AND CATCH THE WISHBONE ON THE OTHER SIDE.

KNEES FLEXED, THE FEET CONTINUE TO PIVOT THE BOARD.

OK! HE ONLY HAS TO REVERSE HIS FEET, ONE IN FRONT OF THE OTHER.

WE WILL STAY NEAR THE SHORE FOR OUR FIRST TRY AT WATERSTART.

LET'S PRACTISE ON A FUNBOARD WHICH DOESN'T SINK.

PUT THE BOARD IN A GOOD POSITION, HEADING OFF THE WIND.

CATCH THE MAST ABOVE YOUR HEAD, THEN POSITION YOURSELF AT THE LEVEL OF THE WISHBONE.

CONTROL THE LIFT OF THE SAIL WITH THE HAND PLACED AT THE FRONT OF THE WISHBONE, OR EVEN ON THE MAST, A LITTLE LOWER.

THE IMPORTANT THING IS TO KEEP THE BODY OFF THE WIND WHILE SWIMMING AND TRYING TO STEP ON THE BOARD.

PUT ONE FOOT ON THE BOARD AND KICK WITH THE OTHER ONE TO RAISE YOURSELF OUT OF THE WATER.

ON LEAVING THE WATER, LEAN ON THE FRONT FOOT TO PREVENT A LUFF.

AND THERE YOU GO! BE SURE TO SECURE ONE FOOT UNDER A STRAP TO AVOID FALLING OVER THE OTHER SIDE.

HOW CAN YOU JUMP SO HIGH ON A WAVE, ERIC?

BY FOLLOWING ITS IMPULSE AT THE RIGHT MOMENT, AT FULL SPEED.

PICK OUT THE WAVE AND CALCULATE ITS POWER.

BEAR OFF IN ORDER TO SAIL OFF THE WIND, AND TO HELP YOU REACH MAXIMUM SPEED.

FEET ON THE RAIL, TAKE THE WAVE'S IMPULSE WITH AN EXTENSION OF THE BACK LEG.

ATTACK THE WAVE STRAIGHT ON, WITH A LIGHT COUNTERLIST.

NOW! THE TAKE OFF!

ONCE IN THE AIR YOU MUST OPEN THE SAIL SO THAT IT WON'T FOLD BACK AND STRAIGHTEN OUT THE BOARD.

ONE MUST LAND WITH THE FRONT OF THE BOARD FIRST AND A LIGHT COUNTER LIST TO AVOID A SKID DURING THE LANDING. ..